SOLACE

PJ Auchterlonie

ISBN 979-8-89112-369-4 (Paperback)
ISBN 979-8-89112-370-0 (Digital)

Covenant Books
11661 Hwy 707
Murrells Inlet, SC 29576
www.covenantbooks.com

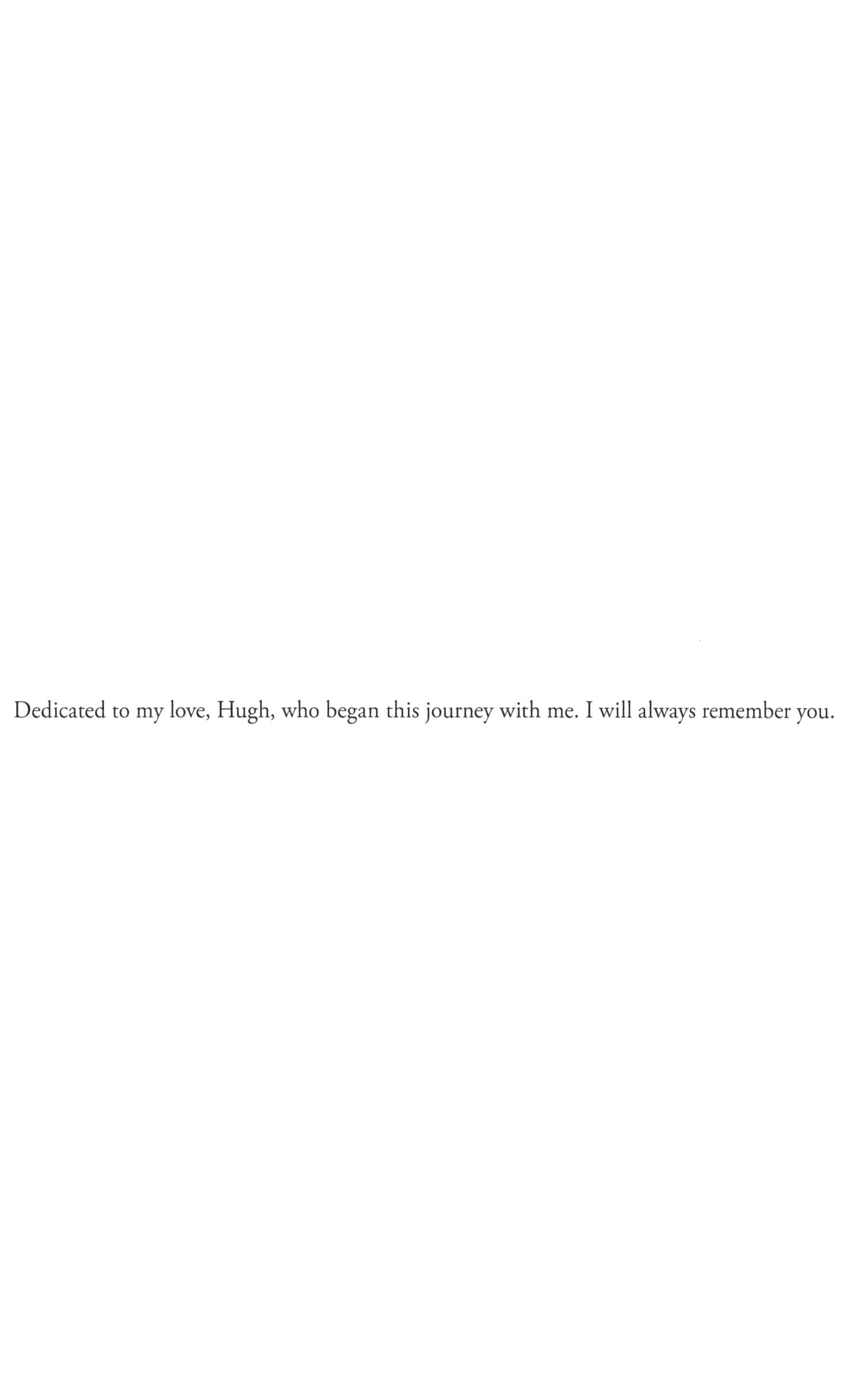

Dedicated to my love, Hugh, who began this journey with me. I will always remember you.

Solace: comfort or consolation in a time of distress or sadness.

Solace was originally written during a time in my life when I was going through a rough patch on the road. My life was filled with numerous activities. I was an elementary teacher and a Sunday school teacher, and I sang in the choir. I had numerous friends and a close-knit family. Then I experienced a divorce and the death of a close friend within a few months of each other. This brought me into a depression for the first time in my life. I sought help through a counselor and a support group. But the comfort or solace from my pain came from within me and through my relationship with God.

That help for me began as I started reading scripture, reflecting on Bible stories that echoed similar pains as my life story and praying daily for myself and others. I found that I was acknowledging my feelings, and despite the pain of reliving those painful feelings, I was experiencing some relief. I began journaling my feelings and my plans for changes and responses to those feelings. This was the beginning of *Solace*.

As I continued to heal in my grieving process, I noticed friends who were also experiencing distress, sadness, or depression as a result of some type of loss. One friend's wife had recently passed away following a lengthy illness. A friend at church had lost her job and was struggling six months later with depression. Another friend was dealing with unresolved issues following the death of his father. While listening to my friends' expressions of grief, I decided to intentionally combine the scripture and journal reflection ideas. I hoped that my scripture themes and journal reflection could serve as solace for others who were experiencing grief.

Solace has been used as an individual reflective journal for people who have been experiencing loss. It also has been used as a church small group event. *Solace* was not designed to move a person through the grief process before they are ready to move to another stage. Rather, *Solace* was designed for each individual to utilize Bible stories and reflective journals to develop their own spiritual journey and to find comfort or consolation in a time of distress or sadness. The design of *Solace* makes it so that it is individualized for each person's needs. What you put into it is what you will get out. How deeply each person invests in their personal life story is entirely up to them.

The format of *Solace* is quite simple. There are seven chapters, with each chapter representing a week's reflection tools. Each chapter's main focus is a theme that will serve as a guidepost on each person's spiritual journey. The beginning of each chapter is a prelude, which is a snippet or snapshot of my life at the time I was experiencing my loss. This reflection from me sets the tone for each chapter and voices the emotions or events that were dominant at that point in my life. Following the prelude is a scripture passage that represents that theme. The next part of the chapter contains reflective questions that will help the reader to describe feelings and responses to a grief experience. Prayer requests and a thematic prayer are the next components to help the reader turn their pain over to God. The chapter ends with a homework assignment to record and reflect on that week's thematic events.

Since my initial writing of *Solace* and its implementation using peer small groups, life brought new changes into my life. I remarried and moved to a different state to work on a revitalization project in a public school. Life felt very meaningful because I had positive relationships and a purposeful job. Then my husband's health suffered, and he died after numerous complications. Three months after he passed, my administrator asked me if I would consider retiring so she could bring on someone younger whom she wanted to hire. Then my father passed away. It felt like I was walking down a dark road that I didn't think I would ever go down again. I found myself not wanting to get out of bed. I was struggling with my identity and whether I was useful to anyone. I had no job to go to, no spouse, and no father. Finding my *Solace* workbook, I read it and began the process of reading the scriptures, answering the questions, and praying actively for myself and others. I have revised some of the content but have found that *Solace* has sustained the test of time. In its new revision, *Solace* has become a book that, while it could serve as a small group tool, is just as effective as a reflective book for individuals. Using *Solace* has helped me find comfort and consolation in my time of loss. I hope it does the same for you.

PJ Auchterlonie

CHAPTER 1

Betrayal

Prelude

While years have passed since he told me about his girlfriend and his plans for divorce, the pain and feeling of betrayal are still very real. In an instant, I am reliving the moment when I heard that very matter-of-fact voice telling me that it's over. I pleaded with him. I bargained. But nothing made any difference. In a matter of weeks, I was packed and moving with my sixteen-year-old son. I thought to myself that I could not get through this. And yet I did. Some days were harder than others, and I felt like I was barely able to hang on. But even on the good days, underneath the surface, that hurt was there. How can we free ourselves of those old hurts? Today, I am ready to feel that pain and name it. God help me as I think about that time and bring that pain to the surface. God help me name this pain so I can finally begin to live my life on my own terms.

When Isaac was old and his eyes were dim so that he could not see, he called Esau his older son, and said to him, "My son"; and he answered, "Here I am." He said, "Behold, I am old; I do not know the day of my death. Now then, take your weapons, your quiver and your bow, and go out to the field, and hunt game for me, and prepare for me savory food, such as I love, and bring it to me that I may eat; that I may bless you before I die." Now Rebekah was listening when Isaac spoke to his son Esau. So when Esau went to the field to hunt for game and bring it, Rebekah said to her son Jacob, "I heard your father speak to your brother Esau,' Bring me game, and prepare for me savory food, that I may eat it, and bless you before the LORD before I die.' Now therefore, my son, obey my word as I command you. Go to the flock, and fetch me two good kids, that I may prepare from them savory food for your father, such as he loves; and you shall bring it to your father to eat, so that he may bless you before he dies."

But Jacob said to Rebekah his mother, "Behold, my brother Esau is a hairy man, and I am a smooth man. Perhaps my father will feel me, and I shall seem to be mocking him, and bring a curse upon myself and not a blessing." His mother said to him, "Upon me be your curse, my son; only obey my word, and go, fetch them to me." So he went and took them and brought them to his mother; and his mother prepared savory food, such as his father loved. Then Rebekah took the best garments of Esau her older son, which were with her in the house, and put them on Jacob her younger son; and the skins of the kids she put upon his hands and upon the smooth part of his neck; and she gave the savory food and the bread, which she had prepared, into the hand of her son Jacob.

So he went in to his father, and said, "My father"; and he said, "Here I am; who are you, my son?" Jacob said to his father, "I am Esau your first-born. I have done as you told me; now sit up and eat of my game, that you may bless me."

But Isaac said to his son, "How is it that you have found it so quickly, my son?" He answered, "Because the LORD your God granted me success." Then Isaac said to Jacob, "Come near, that I may feel you, my son, to know whether you are really my son Esau or not." So Jacob went near to Isaac his father, who felt him and said, "The voice is Jacob's voice, but the hands are the hands of Esau." And he did not recognize him, because his hands were hairy like his brother Esau's hands; so he blessed him. He said, "Are you really my son Esau?" He answered, "I am."

Then he said, "Bring it to me, that I may eat of my son's game and bless you." So he brought it to him, and he ate; and he brought him wine, and he drank. Then his father Isaac said to him, "Come near and kiss me, my son." So he came near and kissed him; and he smelled the smell of his garments, and blessed him, and said, "See, the smell of my son is as the smell of a field which the LORD has blessed! May God give you of the dew of heaven, and of the fatness of the earth, and plenty of grain and wine. Let peoples serve you, and nations bow down to you. Be lord over your brothers, and may your mother's sons bow down to you. Cursed be everyone who curses you, and blessed be everyone who blesses you!"

As soon as Isaac had finished blessing Jacob, when Jacob had scarcely gone out from the presence of Isaac his father, Esau his brother came in from his hunting. He also prepared savory food, and brought it to his father. And he said to his father, "Let my father arise, and eat of his son's game, that you may bless me." His father Isaac said to him, "Who are you?" He answered, "I am your son, your first-born, Esau."

Then Isaac trembled violently, and said, "Who was it then that hunted game and brought it to me, and I ate it all before you came, and I have blessed him? Yes, and he shall be blessed." When Esau heard the words of his father, he cried out with an exceedingly great and bitter cry, and said to his father, "Bless me, even me also, O my father!" But he said, "Your brother came with guile, and he has taken away your blessing." Esau said, "Is he not rightly named Jacob? For he has supplanted me these two times. He took away my birthright; and behold, now he has taken away my blessing." Then he said, "Have you not reserved a blessing for me?"

Isaac answered Esau, "Behold, I have made him your lord, and all his brothers I have given to him for servants, and with grain and wine I have sustained him. What then can I do for you, my son?" Esau said to his father, "Have you but one blessing, my father? Bless me, even me also, O my father." And Esau lifted up his voice and wept. Then Isaac his father answered him: "Behold, away from the fatness of the earth shall your dwelling be, and away from the dew of heaven on high. By your sword you shall live, and you shall serve your brother; but when you break loose you shall break his yoke from your neck."

Now Esau hated Jacob because of the blessing with which his father had blessed him and Esau said to himself, "The days of mourning for my father are approaching; then I will kill my brother Jacob." But the words of Esau her older son were told to Rebekah; so she sent and called Jacob her younger son, and said to him, "Behold, your brother Esau comforts himself by planning to kill you. Now therefore, my son, obey my voice; arise, flee to Laban my brother in Haran, and stay with him a while, until your brother's fury turns away; until your brother's anger turns away, and he forgets what you have done to him; then I will send, and fetch you from there. Why should I be bereft of you both in one day?" (Genesis 27:1–45 Revised Standard Version)

Journal questions:

1. Have you ever felt betrayed by a loved one? Why do you think that happened? Think of the events that happened prior to the betrayal. Think of what happened afterward. Esau is so angry by his brother's betrayal that he vows to kill him. How did you feel in the face of this betrayal? How did you respond to this betrayal?
2. Has there been a time in your life when you have betrayed a loved one? Jacob ran from his brother's anger and did not face him for many years. Think of the feelings from your perspective and the person who you betrayed. Where does your relationship with that person stand now?
3. Following this reflection, who comes to your mind that needs prayers?

Prayer for Betrayal

Dear Lord,

We bring to you today our feelings of anger as we reflect on betrayals, and we turn those feelings over to you. Help us as we begin the process of allowing ourselves to feel and give us the strength to acknowledge our feelings. Surround us with your healing love so that we rest in the assurance that we are not alone. Help us to fill our lives with good, positive activities that help us grow in your love. Lord, we ask for your help not only in our lives but also in those who we bring before you now. Lord be with:

Help those who are sick or troubled, and let them feel your love in their lives. We ask your blessings as we strive to follow your ways. Amen.

Reflections

In the coming week, reflect on your emotions and conflicts within your life. Record all conflicts, especially any that feel like betrayals. Record your emotions and actions during those incidents. After writing those incidents of conflict, think about each situation and how you handled the conflict. Would you change your response or actions?

CHAPTER 2

Pain and Sorrows

Prelude

When my second husband passed away, everyone talked about how brave and in control I was. And I thought I was too. After all, it wasn't a surprise. He had been sick for several months and was hospitalized for twenty-one days before he passed. I called for a hospice program and spent the last days of his life with him. He died with me at his side. And then a few weeks after he passed, I turned to his chair to ask him a question and promptly broke into tears. I continued to be flooded with memories and found myself crying often. It's now been a year. I still cry at times. I miss him. I remember him and all the special times we had together. I think I will always remember him and always feel sad that he is no longer in my life. And I believe that it's okay to feel sad. What I don't want is to feel that my sadness takes over and controls my life.

Jacob dwelt in the land of his father's sojournings, in the land of Canaan. This is the history of the family of Jacob. Joseph, being seventeen years old, was shepherding the flock with his brothers; he was a lad with the sons of Bilhah and Zilpah, his father's wives; and Joseph brought an ill report of them to their father. Now Israel loved Joseph more than any other of his children, because he was the son of his old age; and he made him a long robe with sleeves. But when his brothers saw that their father loved him more than all his brothers, they hated him, and could not speak peaceably to him. Now Joseph had a dream, and when he told it to his brothers they only hated him the more. He said to them, "Hear this dream which I have dreamed: behold, we were binding sheaves in the field, and lo, my sheaf arose and stood upright; and behold, your sheaves gathered round it, and bowed down to my sheaf."

His brothers said to him, "Are you indeed to reign over us? Or are you indeed to have dominion over us?" So they hated him yet more for his dreams and for his words. Then he dreamed another dream, and told it to his brothers, and said, "Behold, I have dreamed another dream; and behold, the sun, the moon, and eleven stars were bowing down to me." But when he told it to his father and to his brothers, his father rebuked him, and said to him, "What is this dream that you have dreamed? Shall I and your mother and your brothers indeed come to bow ourselves to the ground before you?"

And his brothers were jealous of him, but his father kept the saying in mind. Now his brothers went to pasture their father's flock near Shechem. And Israel said to Joseph, "Are not your brothers pasturing the flock at Shechem? Come, I will send you to them." And he said to him, "Here I am." So he said to him, "Go now, see if it is well with your brothers, and with the flock; and bring me word again." So he sent him from the valley of Hebron, and he came to Shechem. And a man found him wandering in the fields; and the man asked him, "What are you seeking?"

"I am seeking my brothers," he said, "tell me, I pray you, where they are pasturing the flock." And the man said, "They have gone away, for I heard them say, 'Let us go to Dothan.'" So Joseph went after his brothers, and found them at Dothan. They saw him afar off, and before he came near to them they conspired against him to kill him. They said to one another, "Here comes this dreamer. Come now, let us kill him and throw him into one of the pits; then we shall say that a wild beast has devoured him, and we shall see what will become of his dreams."

But when Reuben heard it, he delivered him out of their hands, saying, "Let us not take his life." And Reuben said to them, "Shed no blood; cast him into this pit here in the wilderness, but lay no hand upon him"—that he might rescue him out of their hand, to restore him to his father. So when Joseph came to his brothers, they stripped him of his robe, the long robe with sleeves that he wore; and they took him and cast him into a pit. The pit was empty, there was no water in it. Then they sat down to eat; and looking up they saw a caravan of Ish'maelites coming from Gilead, with their camels bearing gum, balm, and myrrh, on their way to carry it down to Egypt.

Then Judah said to his brothers, "What profit is it if we slay our brother and conceal his blood? Come, let us sell him to the Ish'maelites, and let not our hand be upon him, for he is our brother, our own flesh." And his brothers heeded him. Then Mid'ianite traders passed by; and they drew Joseph up and lifted him out of the pit, and sold him to the Ish'maelites for twenty shekels of silver; and they took Joseph to Egypt. When Reuben returned to the pit and saw that Joseph was not in the pit, he rent his clothes and returned to his brothers, and said, "The lad is gone; and I, where shall I go?"

Then they took Joseph's robe, and killed a goat, and dipped the robe in the blood; and they sent the long robe with sleeves and brought it to their father, and said, "This we have found; see now whether it is your son's robe or not." And he recognized it, and said, "It is my son's robe; a wild beast has devoured him; Joseph is without doubt torn to pieces."

Then Jacob rent his garments, and put sackcloth upon his loins, and mourned for his son many days. All his sons and all his daughters rose up to comfort him; but he refused to be comforted, and said, "No, I shall go down to Sheol to my son, mourning." Thus his father wept for him. (Genesis 37:1–35 Revised Standard Version)

Journal questions:

1. Have you felt like a victim such as Joseph? Reflect on the pain in Joseph's life. Joseph's pain started with betrayal and rejection by loved ones and progressed to physical abuse and fear of loss of life. Next, Joseph found himself in a completely unfamiliar life in which he had very little control over his life. Have you experienced any of those situations? What did you do in response to this pain?
2. Jacob's sense of grief over the loss of his son is devastating in verses 34 and 35. Can you identify with Jacob's sorrow because of any pain in your life? What would you tell Jacob based on how you have coped with the pains and sorrow that you have experienced in your life?
3. Following this reflection, who comes to your mind that needs prayers?

Prayer for Pains and Sorrows

Dear Lord,

We come to you today, bringing you our pain and sorrows and asking for you to surround us with your comforting love. Be with us as we allow ourselves to truly grieve and feel the pain that comes with those losses. We bring to you today our feelings of grief and loss and turn them over to you. Guide us in the week ahead so that we will make good choices to better help us to grow in your love. Lord, we ask for your help not only in our lives but also in those who we bring before you now. Lord be with:

Help those who are sick or troubled, and let them feel your love in their lives. We ask your blessings as we strive to follow your ways. AMEN.

Reflections

In the coming week, reflect on feelings of pain and sorrow from your past and present. List those feelings here. What has been your response to those feelings in your life? How do you feel about your responses and actions to the grief in your life?

CHAPTER 3

Coping with Life

Prelude

I reach a point where I feel almost numb. I go through the motions of life, but my senses are dull. I don't even feel like I'm really living. But I get up, and I go to work. I breathe in, and I breathe out. I go to bed and try to sleep. And the next day, I start all over again. Where is the joy in life? What if I went back to my home before? I think about old friends from a happier, simpler time of life. It is tempting to try to go back and start over again. Is that the best thing, or should I try to find peace with where I am now? And then the phone rings, and it's an old friend who was thinking of me. Family and friends reach out to me, and I don't always think to thank them or tell them what they mean to me. A child at school draws a picture for me, and I smile, looking at it. There are people in my life who help me so much by just being in my life. I don't have the answers yet about what I should do, but I know that I have choices. It's time for me to ask some questions and listen to God. Lord, where do you want me now?

In the days when the judges ruled there was a famine in the land, and a certain man of Bethlehem in Judah went to sojourn in the country of Moab, he and his wife and his two sons. The name of the man was Elim'elech and the name of his wife Na'omi, and the names of his two sons were Mahlon and Chil'ion; they were Eph'rathites from Bethlehem in Judah. They went into the country of Moab and remained there. But Elim'elech, the husband of Na'omi, died, and she was left with her two sons. These took Moabite wives; the name of the one was Orpah and the name of the other Ruth. They lived there about ten years; and both Mahlon and Chil'ion died, so that the woman was bereft of her two sons and her husband.

Then she started with her daughters-in-law to return from the country of Moab, for she had heard in the country of Moab that the LORD had visited his people and given them food. So she set out from the place where she was, with her two daughters-in-law, and they went on the way to return to the land of

Judah. But Na'omi said to her two daughters-in-law, "Go, return each of you to her mother's house. May the LORD deal kindly with you, as you have dealt with the dead and with me. The LORD grant that you may find a home, each of you in the house of her husband!" Then she kissed them, and they lifted up their voices and wept.

And they said to her, "No, we will return with you to your people." But Na'omi said, "Turn back, my daughters, why will you go with me? Have I yet sons in my womb that they may become your husbands? Turn back, my daughters, go your way, for I am too old to have a husband. If I should say I have hope, even if I should have a husband this night and should bear sons, would you therefore wait till they were grown? Would you therefore refrain from marrying? No, my daughters, for it is exceedingly bitter to me for your sake that the hand of the LORD has gone forth against me."

Then they lifted up their voices and wept again; and Orpah kissed her mother-in-law, but Ruth clung to her. And she said, "See, your sister-in-law has gone back to her people and to her gods; return after your sister-in-law."

But Ruth said, "Entreat me not to leave you or to return from following you; for where you go I will go, and where you lodge I will lodge; your people shall be my people, and your God my God; where you die I will die, and there will I be buried. May the LORD do so to me and more also if even death parts me from you." And when Na'omi saw that she was determined to go with her, she said no more. So the two of them went on until they came to Bethlehem. And when they came to Bethlehem, the whole town was stirred because of them; and the women said, "Is this Na'omi?"

She said to them, "Do not call me Na'omi, call me Mara, for the Almighty has dealt very bitterly with me. I went away full, and the LORD has brought me back empty. Why call me Na'omi, when the LORD has afflicted me and the Almighty has brought calamity upon me?" So Na'omi returned, and Ruth the Moabitess her daughter-in-law with her, who returned from the country of Moab. And they came to Bethlehem at the beginning of barley harvest. (Ruth 1:1–22 Revised Standard Version)

Journal questions:

1. When faced with the loss of her husband and her two sons, Naomi decided to go back to her home. Have you tried to go back to something familiar or something in your past because of a loss in your life? Describe this and tell whether it has worked positively in your life.
2. Naomi was better able to cope with her grief because of Ruth. Who has helped you to cope with the losses in your life? List the Ruths in your life and write a thank you statement for their support. Now think of who in your life needs you to be a Ruth? What can you do to help them cope with life?
3. Following this reflection, who comes to your mind that needs prayers?

Prayer for Coping with Life

Dear Lord,

We thank you for the many blessings in our lives. We especially thank you for all those people whom you have sent our way when we were in pain or in need of comfort. Bless those people who have made a difference in our lives and help us to remember them in our lives. Help us to reach out to others who are in need. Give us the strength and wisdom to be able to minister, showing others your love through our lives. Guide us in the week ahead so that we will make good choices to better help us to grow in your love. Lord, we ask for your help not only in our lives but also in those who we bring before you now. Lord be with:

Help those who are sick or troubled, and let them feel your love in their lives. We ask for your blessings as we strive to follow your ways. AMEN.

Reflections

During this week, notice the people who help you and make a difference in your life. Thank them and tell them why they are important to you. Record these interactions with the Ruths in your life. Record any incidents when you help others.

CHAPTER 4

Acceptance

Prelude

When she calls me to come see her, I'm not ready for the words that she is ready to tell me. "It's stage four now, and I won't have much longer. I've chosen not to continue with chemo or radiation. I have called hospice."

I am not shocked by the words, but I am so sad. My friend has been sick for a long time. I've known her for about ten years, and she has worked with me in my classroom. When she first got sick, I just knew she was going to get better. She has always been such a fighter and has worked hard for whatever she wanted. And she fought this disease for years. She looks at me and tells me she is ready to go. I am not ready to say goodbye. I want her to continue to fight. I want her to get better. I want life to stay the same.

"Do you know what I want right now?" she asks me. "Ice cream and maybe some caramel sauce."

I go get some for both of us. I eat mine, and she tastes a bite or two of hers.

"This is so good," she tells me. "Will you bring me some more on Friday?"

"And if your peach rose bush still has flowers, will you bring me some?"

I do, and on that Friday, we eat, and we laugh, retelling old stories. I visit my friend for a few more weeks, bringing her flowers and special treats to eat. She gives me the gift of learning how to treasure each moment and how to accept the good with the bad. Lord, thank you for being there for me for both the good and the bad times in my life.

There was a man in the land of Uz, whose name was Job; and that man was blameless and upright, one who feared God, and turned away from evil. There were born to him seven sons and three daughters. He had seven thousand sheep, three thousand camels, five hundred yoke of oxen, and five hundred she-asses, and very many servants; so that this man was the greatest of all the people of the east. His sons used to go and hold a feast in the house of each on his day; and they would send and invite their three sisters to eat and drink with them. And when the days of the feast had run their course, Job would send and sanctify them, and he would rise early in the morning and offer burnt offerings according to the number of them all; for Job said, "It may be that my sons have sinned, and cursed God in their hearts." Thus Job did continually. Now there was a day when the sons of God came to present themselves before the Lord, and Satan also came among them. The Lord said to Satan, "Whence have you come?" Satan answered the Lord, "From going to and fro on the earth, and from walking up and down on it."

And the Lord said to Satan, "Have you considered my servant Job, that there is none like him on the earth, a blameless and upright man, who fears God and turns away from evil?" Then Satan answered the Lord, "Does Job fear God for nought? Hast thou not put a hedge about him and his house and all that he has, on every side? Thou hast blessed the work of his hands, and his possessions have increased in the land. But put forth thy hand now, and touch all that he has, and he will curse thee to thy face."

And the Lord said to Satan, "Behold, all that he has is in your power; only upon himself do not put forth your hand." So Satan went forth from the presence of the Lord. Now there was a day when his sons and daughters were eating and drinking wine in their eldest brother's house; and there came a messenger to Job, and said, "The oxen were plowing and the asses feeding beside them; and the Sabe'ans fell upon them and took them, and slew the servants with the edge of the sword; and I alone have escaped to tell you."

While he was yet speaking, there came another, and said, "The fire of God fell from heaven and burned up the sheep and the servants, and consumed them; and I alone have escaped to tell you." While he was yet speaking, there came another, and said, "The Chalde'ans formed three companies, and made a raid upon the camels and took them, and slew the servants with the edge of the sword; and I alone have escaped to tell you." While he was yet speaking, there came another, and said, "Your sons and daughters were eating and drinking wine in their eldest brother's house; and behold, a great wind came across the wilderness, and struck the four corners of the house, and it fell upon the young people, and they are dead; and I alone have escaped to tell you."

Then Job arose, and rent his robe, and shaved his head, and fell upon the ground, and worshiped. And he said, "Naked I came from my mother's womb, and naked shall I return; the Lord gave, and the LORD has taken away; blessed be the name of the Lord."**22**In all this Job did not sin or charge God with wrong. (Job 1:1–22 Revised Standard Version)

Again there was a day when the sons of God came to present themselves before the Lord, and Satan also came among them to present himself before the Lord. And the Lord said to Satan, "Whence have you come?" Satan answered the Lord, "From going to and fro on the earth, and from walking up and down on it." And the Lord said to Satan, "Have you considered my servant Job, that there is none like him on the earth, a blameless and upright man, who fears God and turns away from evil? He still holds fast his integrity, although you moved me against him, to destroy him without cause."

Then Satan answered the Lord, "Skin for skin! All that a man has he will give for his life. But put forth thy hand now, and touch his bone and his flesh, and he will curse thee to thy face." And the Lord said to Satan, "Behold, he is in your power; only spare his life." So Satan went forth from the presence of the Lord, and afflicted Job with loathsome sores from the sole of his foot to the crown of his head. And he took a potsherd with which to scrape himself, and sat among the ashes.

Then his wife said to him, "Do you still hold fast your integrity? Curse God, and die." But he said to her, "You speak as one of the foolish women would speak. Shall we receive good at the hand of God, and shall we not receive evil?" In all this Job did not sin with his lips. Now when Job's three friends heard of all this evil that had come upon him, they came each from his own place, Eli'phaz the Te'manite, Bildad the Shuhite, and Zophar the Na'amathite. They made an appointment together to come to condole with him and comfort him. And when they saw him from afar, they did not recognize him; and they raised their voices and wept; and they rent their robes and sprinkled dust upon their heads toward heaven. And they sat with him on the ground seven days and seven nights, and no one spoke a word to him, for they saw that his suffering was very great. (Job 2:1–13)

Journal questions:

1. Job's friends came to offer him sympathy, but when they saw how great his loss was, they had no words for him. How can you explain when bad things happen to good people?
2. Job tells his wife that if we accept good things from God, then we must also accept the bad things that come. Can you think of events that have been painful to you that you have learned to accept? How did you reach your acceptance?
3. Following this reflection, who comes to your mind that needs prayers?

Prayer for Acceptance

Dear Lord,

We come to you today asking for your strength as we travel on this journey towards acceptance. Be with us as we find ourselves overwhelmed by the pains of our past. Comfort us and help us to lean on you as we take each day one at a time. Surround us with your healing love so that we know that we are not alone. Help us to fill our lives with good, positive activities that help us to grow in your love. Lord, we ask for your help not only in our lives but also in those who we bring before you now. Lord be with:

Help those who are sick or troubled, and let them feel your love in their lives. We ask for your blessings as we strive to follow your ways. AMEN.

Reflections

In this week, reflect on ways that you have accepted painful times in your life and accepted them by moving on with your life in a positive manner. List the positive things that mark your acceptance of those times. Think about new ways that you can continue in your journey of acceptance. List those ideas here.

CHAPTER 5

Guilt and Forgiveness

Prelude

Guilt is the hardest emotion for me to talk about to others. Guilt is the feeling that I live with every day, and I know it like it's a part of me. And I'm not talking about unrealistic guilt where I blame myself for things that happened for which I wasn't responsible. No, I'm talking about those things I've done that are just plain ugly. I wake up in the morning with that first thought of the day being about my guilt. It follows me everywhere. I see it in my eyes when I look in the mirror. I cannot escape it. Lord, take this burden from me. And yet, since I carry guilt with me as a constant companion, why am I so slow to forgive others? Why can't I put aside the hurts and let them go? I'm not allowing someone to continue to hurt me. I just want to forgive what happened in the past and move on. But I don't do a good job of this. I don't forgive myself, and I don't forgive others. Lord, be with me and help me remember that you have forgiven all my sins. Help me to forgive also.

And he said, "There was a man who had two sons; and the younger of them said to his father, 'Father, give me the share of property that falls to me.' And he divided his living between them. Not many days later, the younger son gathered all he had and took his journey into a far country, and there he squandered his property in loose living. And when he had spent everything, a great famine arose in that country, and he began to be in want. So he went and joined himself to one of the citizens of that country, who sent him into his fields to feed swine. And he would gladly have fed on the pods that the swine ate; and no one gave him anything. But when he came to himself he said, 'How many of my father's hired servants have bread enough and to spare, but I perish here with hunger! I will arise and go to my father, and I will say to him, "Father, I have sinned against heaven and before you; I am no longer worthy to be called your son; treat me as one of your hired servants." 'And he arose and came to his father. But while he was yet at a distance, his father saw him and had compassion, and ran and embraced him and kissed him. And the son said to him, 'Father, I have sinned against heaven and before you; I am no longer worthy to be called your son.'

But the father said to his servants, 'Bring quickly the best robe, and put it on him; and put a ring on his hand, and shoes on his feet; and bring the fatted calf and kill it, and let us eat and make merry; for this my son was dead, and is alive again; he was lost, and is found.' And they began to make merry."

Now his elder son was in the field; and as he came and drew near to the house, he heard music and dancing. And he called one of the servants and asked what this meant. And he said to him, 'Your brother has come, and your father has killed the fatted calf, because he has received him safe and sound.' But he was angry and refused to go in. His father came out and entreated him, but he answered his father, 'Lo, these many years I have served you, and I never disobeyed your command; yet you never gave me a kid, that I might make merry with my friends.

But when this son of yours came, who has devoured your living with harlots, you killed for him the fatted calf!' And he said to him, 'Son, you are always with me, and all that is mine is yours. It was fitting to make merry and be glad, for this your brother was dead, and is alive; he was lost, and is found.'" (Luke 15:11–32 Revised Standard Version)

Journal questions:

1. Guilt and forgiveness are separate but interconnected themes in this passage. Think about times in your life when you feel guilt because of a time when you have hurt someone. Have you been able to ask for their forgiveness? (There are often situations when that is not possible). In the space, list below how you hurt the person and then ask them for forgiveness. Think about the difference between assumed guilt and true guilt. Sometimes, we assume guilt for a situation that is not realistic. An example of unrealistic guilt would be, 'If only I had paid more attention to my mother's symptoms, I would have got her to the doctor sooner, and she wouldn't have died." Be sure that what you are asking for forgiveness is not an example of unrealistic guilt.

2. Forgiveness frees all people involved from old hurts. In this passage, the older brother is unable to experience the joy of reconciliation because he is not able to put his anger and resentment aside. Forgiving does not mean that we have to live with that person or allow them to continue to hurt us. It simply means that we forgive the old hurts and move on from that situation. Is there someone who you have not been able to forgive? What is stopping you from being able to forgive them? If you are ready to begin the process of forgiving them, outline the steps that you plan to take towards forgiving the old hurts within your life.

3. Following this reflection, who comes to your mind that needs prayers?

Prayer for Guilt and Forgiveness

Dear Lord,

We ask your help as we work on old hurts and pain. Help us to forgive those who have hurt us. We ask that the burden of old pains be lifted from our hearts and that we be freed from this baggage. Help us to let it all go. We also ask that you forgive us for all the pain and suffering that we have brought to ourselves and others in our lives. Give us the strength to do what we can to make amends for any wrongs that we have done. Surround us with your healing love so that we know we are not alone. Help us to fill our lives with good, positive activities that help us to grow in your love. Lord, we ask for your help not only in our lives but also in those who we bring before you now. Lord be with:

Help those who are sick or troubled, and let them feel your love in their lives. We ask for your blessings as we strive to follow your ways. AMEN.

Reflections

During the week ahead, think about old hurts in your life. List any plans that you have to begin making amends or initiations toward a healing relationship with others or with yourself. Write down any interactions and the results of those interactions. Are they positive? Do you feel healing is taking place in your life? Are you in reconciliation with God? This may be the time when you ask God for forgiveness for your past actions and begin healing in that aspect. This may be the time when you forgive yourself for any past wrongs.

CHAPTER 6

A Loving God

Prelude

I have been so caught up in my life that I haven't given God much thought lately. I have forgotten to pray. I think about that, and then I remember how faithful God has been to me. I remember one day being at my lowest. I was in the car driving from one side of town to the other, and the whole time, I was thinking about my problems. I remember being focused on a part of my life that I felt powerless to change. And the more I thought about it, the more depressed I became. I was so absorbed with how unhappy I was until a blaring horn blasted me to the present. A little red car was honking loudly behind me. They passed me and cut very tightly right in front of me. I slammed on my brakes to avoid hitting them and noticed their vanity car tags. Godlvsu. I looked at those letters for a few seconds before they registered. God loves you. I had to laugh at that time. God, you are faithful to me and remind me of your presence in my life even when I am totally absorbed in my own problems. And what a sense of humor you have, God. Thank you for sending a bad driver with an attitude to wake me up from my doldrums. Thank you, God, for your faithfulness.

Now Eli'jah the Tishbite, of Tishbe in Gilead, said to Ahab, "As the Lord the God of Israel lives, before whom I stand, there shall be neither dew nor rain these years, except by my word." And the word of the Lord came to him, "Depart from here and turn eastward, and hide yourself by the brook Cherith, that is east of the Jordan. You shall drink from the brook, and I have commanded the ravens to feed you there." So he went and did according to the word of the Lord; he went and dwelt by the brook Cherith that is east of the Jordan. And the ravens brought him bread and meat in the morning, and bread and meat in the evening; and he drank from the brook. And after a while the brook dried up, because there was no rain in the land. Then the word of the Lord came to him, "Arise, go to Zar'ephath, which belongs to Sidon, and dwell there. Behold, I have commanded a widow there to feed you."

So he arose and went to Zar'ephath; and when he came to the gate of the city, behold, a widow was there gathering sticks; and he called to her and said, "Bring me a little water in a vessel that I may drink." And as she was going to bring it, he called to her and said, "Bring me a morsel of bread in your hand." And she said, "As the Lord your God lives, I have nothing baked, only a handful of meal in a jar, and a little oil in a cruse; and now, I am gathering a couple of sticks, that I may go in and prepare it for myself and my son, that we may eat it, and die." And Eli'jah said to her, "Fear not; go and do as you have said; but first make me a little cake of it and bring it to me, and afterward make for yourself and your son. For thus says the Lord the God of Israel, 'The jar of meal shall not be spent, and the cruse of oil shall not fail, until the day that the Lord sends rain upon the earth.'"

And she went and did as Eli'jah said; and she, and he, and her household ate for many days. The jar of meal was not spent, neither did the cruse of oil fail, according to the word of the Lord which he spoke by Eli'jah. After this the son of the woman, the mistress of the house, became ill; and his illness was so severe that there was no breath left in him. And she said to Eli'jah, "What have you against me, O man of God? You have come to me to bring my sin to remembrance, and to cause the death of my son!"

And he said to her, "Give me your son." And he took him from her bosom, and carried him up into the upper chamber, where he lodged, and laid him upon his own bed. And he cried to the Lord, "O Lord my God, hast thou brought calamity even upon the widow with whom I sojourn, by slaying her son?" Then he stretched himself upon the child three times, and cried to the Lord, "O Lord my God, let this child's soul come into him again." And the Lord hearkened to the voice of Eli'jah; and the soul of the child came into him again, and he revived. And Eli'jah took the child, and brought him down from the upper chamber into the house, and delivered him to his mother; and Eli'jah said, "See, your son lives." And the woman said to Eli'jah, "Now I know that you are a man of God, and that the word of the Lord in your mouth is truth." (1 Kings 17:1–24)

Journal questions:

1. Miracles and the assurance of God's love abound in this passage. When the woman has despaired of any hope, God intervenes and saves her and her son from starving to death. Then her son dies, and God brings him back to life with the intercession of Elijah. Has God worked miracles in your life? List them here and reflect on times when you felt immersed in God's love.
2. God loves us and cares for us in so many ways. Sometimes, we forget to thank him for the many ways he has shown us his love. And sometimes we are afraid to ask him for help in our lives. Write a prayer of thanks for God's many gifts in your life. Now add a request for help in an area that you would like to be touched by God's caring and love.
3. Following this reflection, who comes to your mind that needs prayers?

Prayer for a Loving God

Dear Lord,

We thank you for your faithful love and compassion. Throughout all our heartaches and struggles, we know that you have gone every step with us. We ask for your continued blessings and ask that you may direct us to reach out to others so that they may feel your love through us. Lord, we ask for your help not only in our lives but also in those who we bring before you now. Lord be with:

Help those who are sick or troubled, and let them feel your love in their lives. We ask for your blessings as we strive to follow your ways. Amen.

Reflections

Look for evidence of God's caring love for you this week. List the people that God uses to intervene on your behalf. List the events that happened to you this week that show you God's love.

CHAPTER 7

Walking with Jesus

Prelude

I enjoy walking. I've never been a runner in my life and never regretted missing that kind of physical exertion and discipline. But I do find joy in walking. I like to focus on the landscape, the terrain, and the wildlife that can be seen while walking in the country. I like to watch the colors play across the sky with a dramatic sunrise or sunset. I like walking with a dog and feeling the pull of the leash as she shows me the direction that she wants to go. And I like walking with a friend and talking as we share what is going on in our lives. Sometimes, that friend is Jesus. I've found that some days, it's easier to pray while walking and enjoying the outdoors than in church. Lord, help me to be more faithful in my walking with you.

That very day two of them were going to a village named Emmaus, about seven miles from Jerusalem, and talking with each other about all these things that had happened. While they were talking and discussing together, Jesus himself drew near and went with them. But their eyes were kept from recognizing him. And he said to them, "What is this conversation which you are holding with each other as you walk?" And they stood still, looking sad. Then one of them, named Cle'opas, answered him, "Are you the only visitor to Jerusalem who does not know the things that have happened there in these days?"

And he said to them, "What things?" And they said to him, "Concerning Jesus of Nazareth, who was a prophet mighty in deed and word before God and all the people, and how our chief priests and rulers delivered him up to be condemned to death, and crucified him. But we had hoped that he was the one to redeem Israel. Yes, and besides all this, it is now the third day since this happened. Moreover, some women of our company amazed us. They were at the tomb early in the morning and did not find his body; and they came back saying that they had even seen a vision of angels, who said that he was alive. Some of those who were with us went to the tomb, and found it just as the women had said; but him they did not see."

And he said to them, "O foolish men, and slow of heart to believe all that the prophets have spoken! Was it not necessary that the Christ should suffer these things and enter into his glory?" And beginning with Moses and all the prophets, he interpreted to them in all the scriptures the things concerning himself. So they drew near to the village to which they were going. He appeared to be going further, but they constrained him, saying, "Stay with us, for it is toward evening and the day is now far spent." So he went in to stay with them.

When he was at table with them, he took the bread and blessed, and broke it, and gave it to them. And their eyes were opened and they recognized him; and he vanished out of their sight.

They said to each other, "Did not our hearts burn within us while he talked to us on the road, while he opened to us the scriptures?" And they rose that same hour and returned to Jerusalem; and they found the eleven gathered together and those who were with them, who said, "The Lord has risen indeed, and has appeared to Simon!" Then they told what had happened on the road, and how he was known to them in the breaking of the bread. (Luke 24:13–35 Revised Standard Version)

Journal questions:

1. The disciples were discouraged and confused on their journey when Jesus appeared before them. Although he had been so important to them in their lives, now they did not even recognize him. Think of times in your spiritual journey when you have been discouraged and confused. Did you recognize Jesus's presence in your life? Reflect on those times.
2. Are you walking with Jesus now in your spiritual journey? List the ways that you experience the risen Lord in your daily life. Then make a list of how you would like to add more time with Jesus in your life.
3. Following this reflection, who comes to your mind that needs prayers?

Prayer for Walking with Jesus

Dear Lord,

We thank you for your daily presence in our lives. Throughout all our heartaches and struggles, we know that you have been walking with us. We ask for your continued blessings and ask that you direct us to reach out to others so that they may feel your love through us. Lord, we ask for your help not only in our lives but also in those who we bring before you now. Lord be with:

Help those who are sick or troubled, and let them feel your love in their lives. We ask for your blessings as we strive to follow your ways. Amen.

Reflections

As you come to the end of this reflective journey, you realize that you have been traveling a road that has had many mileposts representing your spiritual journey. Go back and read your previous reflections. Have you changed with these reflections? How do you want to continue to grow? What do you need to make that happen? And now you realize that this is not the end but only the beginning. This is your journal and will continue to show you signposts on your spiritual journey. Take it out and add to it throughout your life. The changes and reflections will guide you on your way. God bless you.

ABOUT THE AUTHOR

PJ Auchterlonie is a retired early childhood teacher who lives in Wichita, Kansas. Through her own life experiences, PJ wrote *Solace*, a reflective journal to help herself and others on their grief journey. This is her first book.

9 7 9 8 8 9 1 1 2 3 6 9 4